D1742921

Life of Bailey

A True Life Story:

Living in a Pandemic

Sensei Paul David

COPYRIGHT PAGE

Life of Bailey: A True Life Story: Living In A Pandemic
by Sensei Paul David,

Copyright © 2021.

All rights reserved.

978-1-990106-77-4 - Living In A Pandemic - Hardcover Book

978-1-990106-76-7 - Living In A Pandemic - Paperback Book

978-1-990106-75-0 – Living In A Pandemic - Electronic Book

This book is not authorized for free distribution copying.

SENSEI PUBLISHING

It's A Great Day To Be Alive!

www.senseipublishing.com

@senseipublishing
#senseipublishing

Get Our FREE Books Now!

FREE Kids Books

lifeofbailey.senseipublishing.com

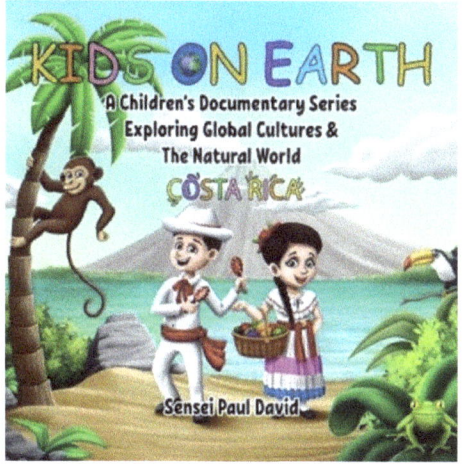

kidsonearth.senseipublishing.com

FREE Self-Development Book for Every Family

senseiselfdevelopment.senseipublishing.com

Click Below or Search Amazon for Another Book In Each Series Or Visit:

www.amazon.com/author/senseipauldavid

Join Our Publishing Journey!

If you would like to receive FUTURE FREE BOOKS and get to know us better, please click www.senseipublishing.com and join our newsletter by entering your email address in the pop-up box.

Follow Our Blog: senseipauldavid.ca

Follow/Like/Subscribe: Facebook, Instagram, YouTube: @senseipublishing

Scan the QR Code with your phone or tablet

to follow us on social media: Like / Subscribe / Follow

Daddy and Mommy were going on a vacation, and Bailey needed a place to stay while Daddy and Mommy were gone. So Daddy and Mommy took Bailey to stay at the dog walker's house while they were gone.

Bailey already knew the dog walker and was happy to see her again. The dog Walker had a big pet bunny rabbit for Bailey to play with, and while Bailey was busy playing with the bunny, Daddy and Mommy waved to the dog Walker and left.

Many days went by. While Bailey was playing in the backyard of the dog walker's house, Bailey missed Daddy and Mommy but felt safe.

One morning, the dog Walker brought 3 new dog friends for Bailey to play in the backyard. Bailey had lots of fun running around the yard with his new friends.

When Daddy and Mommy got home from their vacation, they came to pick Bailey up from the dog walker's house. Daddy called loudly, 'Bailey, where's Daddy?'

Bailey ran towards Daddy and started licking his face. Bailey was so excited that he nearly knocked Daddy over. Mommy hugged the dog Walker and said 'thank you for taking care of our big boy.' The dog Walker said, 'Welcome home! Bailey was such a good dog.'

A few days passed, and Daddy and Mommy were watching the news on TV in the living room. Bailey watched as Daddy and Mommy looked very serious and a little bit worried. This made Bailey feel nervous too.

8

After a while, Bailey followed Daddy and Mommy to the kitchen and watched as they started talking to each other. They looked very serious. Daddy told Mommy, 'This news could change our lives for a long time, and we need to keep safe.' Mommy said, 'I agree, I hope things go back to normal soon.'

Bailey did not understand what Daddy and Mommy were talking about, but he knew that something very serious was happening.

A few days later, Bailey noticed that things were changing. Daddy and Mommy were watching the news on TV instead of playing outside with Bailey. This made Bailey feel sad and confused.

12

Days turned into weeks when Bailey noticed that Mommy and Daddy were spending every day indoors, sitting in front of their computers.

Bailey felt upset and missed his parents' love. All Bailey wanted was for Mommy and Daddy to play outside with him like normal.

14

A week later, Bailey felt like it was time to tell his Daddy how he was feeling.

So, when Daddy was working on his computer, Bailey gently put his paw on Daddy's foot, but Daddy didn't seem to notice and kept working. This made Bailey feel even more upset.

One day when Daddy and Mommy took Bailey for a walk, Bailey noticed how everyone looked different now. People were wearing big masks to cover their faces.

Even Daddy and Mommy were wearing face masks. Bailey wondered what these were used for and why everybody was wearing them.

The next day at the dog park, Bailey ran over to some other dogs and people to say hello. Bailey was always very friendly in the dog park. But this time Daddy kept calling for Bailey to come back to him.

Bailey listened to Daddy but could not understand why Daddy wanted him to stay away from the other dogs and people.

Weeks passed by, and Bailey became bored and lonely because Daddy and Mommy didn't take Bailey outside as much anymore. All Bailey wanted was to be outside, and this made Bailey very upset.

22

Bailey did not know how else to tell Daddy how he was feeling. Daddy and Mommy looked so busy and stressed, and Bailey didn't want to bother them. So Bailey cried to himself while Mommy and Daddy worked.

24

Early the next morning Daddy said, 'Come on Bailey, it's time to visit the sailing club!' Bailey was so excited to go on another adventure with Daddy, but when they got to the sailing club, there was no one there to talk to. Daddy and Bailey felt lonely, even though they were at the sailing club.

The next evening, Daddy, Mommy, and Bailey went for a walk in the city. Bailey noticed that no people were walking around on the streets and that all the stores were closed and empty. Bailey could see that Mommy and Daddy were feeling uncomfortable.

The next day, Bailey looked out of the window and wondered why his life had changed so much all of a sudden.

Bailey was used to going on so many adventures and exploring the city, and now everything was different. Daddy and Mommy seemed to be so busy all of the time. So, Bailey decided to try to tell Daddy how he felt again.

That night, while Daddy was watching the news on TV, Bailey hopped up on Daddy's lap and started barking very loudly. Daddy was shocked by how Bailey was acting!

Then Bailey jumped off Daddy's lap and ran over to the front door. Bailey started crying and barking at the door while looking back at Daddy on the couch. Daddy could see that Bailey was trying to tell him something.

34

This time, Daddy realized that Bailey was trying to speak to him and that Bailey needed more attention. Daddy went over to Bailey by the front door to comfort him. Daddy told Bailey, 'I'm so sorry that our life has changed Bailey, but this also means that we can change to make things better.' Daddy promised Bailey that they would figure this out together, as a family.

36

Later that night, Daddy went to speak to Mommy in the kitchen and Bailey followed. Daddy told Mommy, 'This pandemic is very serious, but it can't stop us from enjoying our life.'

'From now on, let's find new and safe ways to go on adventures.' Mommy and Bailey smiled at Daddy. Bailey could sense Daddy and Mommy felt better, and Bailey felt better too.

A few days later, Daddy and Mommy took Bailey on a water taxi to visit Toronto Island. Bailey loved feeling the fast fresh air blowing in his face as the boat moved across the water.

40

Daddy and Mommy rented two bicycles and took Bailey on the bike trails by the beach.

Daddy tossed a frisbee into the lake and Bailey quickly ran after it, while Mommy took pictures of Bailey. Bailey loved splashing around in the water, and spending time with his Mommy and Daddy outside!

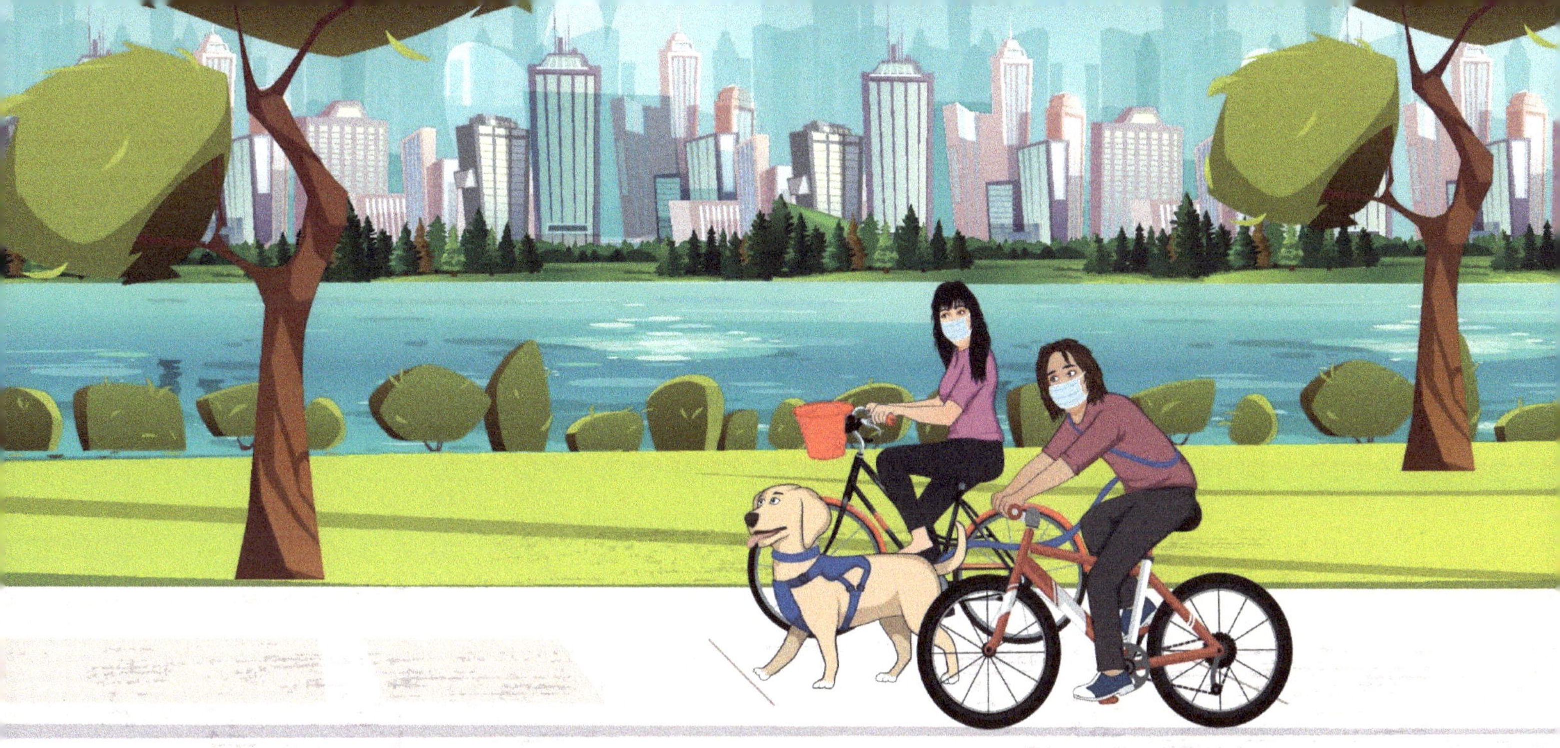

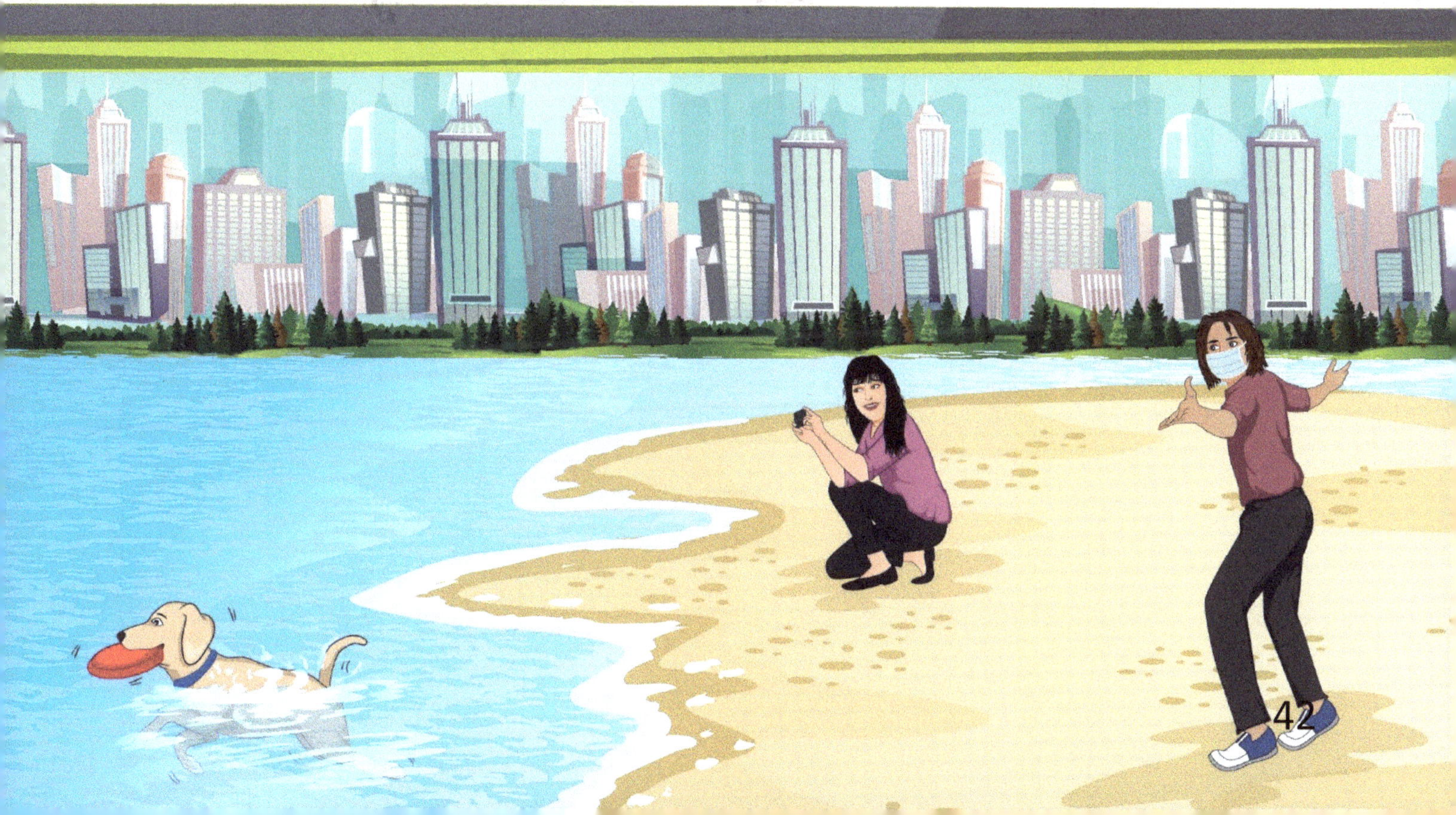

Bailey was tired after the busy day, and as soon as they got home, Bailey went straight to his bed and fell asleep. That night, Bailey dreamt about how happy Daddy and Mommy made him feel that day.

When Bailey woke up in the morning, it was pouring with rain and was very cold. Daddy and Bailey did not want to walk outside for very long, because they did not like to get too wet.

So, after a short walk in the rain, Daddy ran up and down the stairs with Bailey following him, over and over again! Bailey needed the exercise and loved to follow Daddy.

46

Some days, Daddy and Mommy would take a break from their work and toss a ball to each other for Bailey to chase. Bailey felt like he was a part of the family again, and because he could tell that Daddy and Mommy were happy again, so was he.

On days when Daddy and Mommy were too busy to play with Bailey, Daddy hid treats in Bailey's ball. It was Bailey's job to get the treats out of the ball!

After some time, Bailey realized that when he chewed the ball, little bits of treats would come out. This kept Bailey busy, and he had lots of fun with his treat ball. Now, he was just as busy as Mommy and Daddy!

Daddy started to teach Bailey how to speak using a voice button.

When Bailey pressed the voice button, the button said 'Outside.' Now Bailey could tell Daddy when he wanted to go outside. Mommy was so excited when Bailey learned how to use the voice button and hoped that one day, Bailey would learn to talk!

One sunny morning in the kitchen, Mommy video-called her mother, who was called 'Mimi.' Mimi was feeling lonely because she lived alone and life had changed for her too. Daddy could hear that Mimi was feeling sad, and so Daddy told Mimi that she should get a puppy to keep her company.

When Bailey walked in and wagged his tail to Mimi over the phone, Mimi and Mommy thought that this was a great idea. Mimi said that she would start to look for a puppy to adopt!

Not long after, Mimi adopted a new puppy named Chico. Chico was very small compared to Bailey. He had white and brown fluffy fur, floppy ears, and was very playful.

Daddy, Mommy, and Bailey went to meet Mimi and Chico at the sailing club, where everyone could be together outside.

Fall started and it felt cooler outside. Chico had grown a bit bigger and was now strong enough to join Mommy, Daddy, and Bailey on a hike.

Mimi let Mommy and Daddy take Chico to a Forest where Bailey and his new Cousin Chico could run free and play on their own.

They ran in circles around Mommy and Daddy as they took turns chasing one another. Bailey loved playing with his new little cousin!

On the drive home from the hike in the Forest, Bailey and Chico fell asleep next to each other in the back seat of the car.

While Daddy was driving, he said to Mommy, 'The Pandemic gave Bailey a new cousin to play with, and it gave Mimi a friend to keep her company. It also gave us new ways to spend time together as a family.'

Daddy replied to Mommy, 'I'm not sure when life will go back to the way it used to be, but now I know that when times change, we can change too, and we can still have adventures. I wonder what new adventures we will think of next?'

Mommy turned to Daddy and said, 'It's a great day to be alive!'

A Puppy Adventure for the Ages - Living in a Pandemic

When a worldwide Pandemic starts to change life for Bailey and his Daddy and Mommy, the happy family is forced to get used to living life a different way. When Bailey is not allowed to play with other dogs and people, and rather spends his days inside, Bailey struggles to understand why his life is changing. After he learns how to talk to Mommy and Daddy about how he is feeling, Bailey learns that there are always new adventures to be had. Follow along as our favourite service dog and his Mommy and Daddy learn how to change their day-to-day lives and still have fun and go on adventures, in the time of a Pandemic.

Don't miss out on the chance to follow Bailey and his family as they learn to live in the time of a pandemic, in 'Life of Bailey - Living in a Pandemic!'

Sensei Publishing provides kids with a series of books for generations of people, encouraging exciting curiosity and interactive discovery.

Join Our Publishing Journey! Get FREE Books & FREE Guided Meditations for Kids, Special Offers, and much more! Visit www.senseipublishing.com Today!

You're all invited to take a look behind the scenes and experience our creative process - Learn about our new books by subscribing to our newsletter.

Follow, Like, Share, and Subscribe on Facebook and Instagram at @lifeofbailey and on
YouTube and Google Search at #senseipublishing

- It's a great day to be alive!

Thank you for reading this book!

If you found this book helpful, I would be grateful if you would **post an honest review on Amazon** so this book can reach other supportive readers like you!

All you need to do is digitally flip to the back and leave your review. Or visit amazon.com/author/senseipauldavid click the correct book cover and click on the blue link next to the yellow stars that say, "customer reviews."

As always...

It's a great day to be alive!

Get/Share Our FREE All-Ages Mental Health Books Now!

FREE Kids Books

lifeofbailey.senseipublishing.com

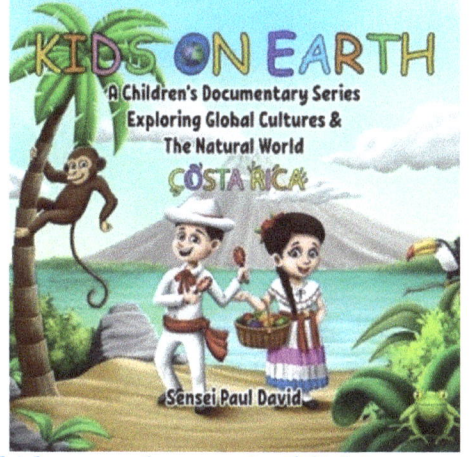

kidsonearth.senseipublishing.com

FREE Self-Development Book for Every Family

senseiselfdevelopment.senseipublishing.com

Click Below or Search Amazon for Another Book In Each Series Or Visit:

www.amazon.com/author/senseipauldavid

www.senseipublishing.com

@senseipublishing
#senseipublishing

Check out our **recommendations** for other books for adults &
kids plus other great resources by visiting
www.senseipublishing.com/resources/

Join Our Publishing Journey!

If you would like to receive FREE BOOKS, special offers, please visit
www.senseipublishing.com and join our newsletter by entering your email address in the
pop-up box

Follow Our Engaging Blog NOW!
senseipauldavid.ca

Get Our FREE Books Today!

Click & Share the Links Below

FREE Kids Books
lifeofbailey.senseipublishing.com
kidsonearth.senseipublishing.com

FREE Self-Development Book

senseiselfdevelopment.senseipublishing.com

FREE BONUS!!!
Experience Over 25 FREE Engaging Guided Meditations!

Prized Skills & Practices for Adults & Kids. Help Restore Deep-Sleep, Lower Stress, Improve Posture, Navigate Uncertainty & More.

Download the Free Insight Timer App and click the link below:
http://insig.ht/sensei_paul

If you like these meditations & want to go deeper email me for a FREE 30min LIVE Coaching Session:
senseipauldavid@senseipublishing.com

About Sensei Publishing

Sensei Publishing commits itself to help people of all ages transform into better versions of themselves by providing high-quality and research-based self-development books with an emphasis on mental health and guided meditations. Sensei Publishing offers well-written e-books, audiobooks, paperbacks and online courses that simplify complicated but practical topics in line with its mission to inspire people towards positive transformation.

It's a great day to be alive!

About the Author

I create simple & transformative eBooks & Guided Meditations for Adults & Children proven to help navigate uncertainty, solve niche problems & bring families closer together.

I'm a former finance project manager, private pilot, jiu-jitsu instructor, musician & former University of Toronto Fitness Trainer. I prefer a science-based approach to focus on these & other areas in my life to stay humble & hungry to evolve. I hope you enjoy my work and I'd love to hear your feedback.

- It's a great day to be alive!
Sensei Paul David

Scan & Follow/Like/Subscribe: Facebook, Instagram, YouTube: @senseipublishing

Scan using your phone/iPad camera for Social Media

Visit us at www.senseipublishing.com and sign up for our newsletter to learn more about our exciting books and to experience our FREE Guided Meditations for Kids & Adults.

Lightning Source UK Ltd.
Milton Keynes UK
UKHW052213250821
389455UK00002B/49